T0208965

Unveil the Reality

28 Daily Devotionals from The Book of Acts

NORKA JENKINS
&
TAYLER JENKINS

WESTBOW
PRESS®
A DIVISION OF THOMAS NELSON
& ZONDERVAN

WestBow Press books may be ordered through booksellers or by contacting:

WestBow Press
A Division of Thomas Nelson & Zondervan
1663 Liberty Drive
Bloomington, IN 47403
www.westbowpress.com
844-714-3454

ISBN: 978-1-6642-3692-9 (sc)
ISBN: 978-1-6642-3693-6 (hc)
ISBN: 978-1-6642-3691-2 (e)

Library of Congress Control Number: 2021911858

Print information available on the last page.

WestBow Press rev. date: 06/24/2021

CONTENTS

How to Use this Book

In order to maximize your experience while reading this devotional, we encourage you to prepare your heart to hear from the Lord through prayer. Ask the Lord to clear your mind of any distractions, grant you His wisdom, and open your heart to the truth of His word. With your Bible handy, allow the word of God to minister to you as you read the corresponding chapter in Acts for each of the next twenty-eight days. After reading the chapter of the day, simply thank the Lord for the reading of His word, open this book, and turn to the corresponding devotional for the day.

Each day begins with a short excerpt from the daily chapter reading and then expounds on the selected reference in the body of the devotional. Each verse is analyzed in light of its scriptural context while simultaneously highlighting its present-day relevance and application. In a separate journal or in the space provided at the end of each chapter, feel free to note what resonates most with you from the reading. At the end of each devotional reading are reflection questions that have been carefully crafted to inspire practical application. The word of God encourages us to not only be hearers of the word, but doers as well (see James 1:22–25). Refrain from providing simple yes or no responses, but allow the Holy Spirit to guide you in greater depth when answering each question. Your responses will be the key to walking in the reality of a transformed life in Christ. Finally, at the end of every chapter is a declaration prayer. Infused with the word of God, the prayer encourages you to speak aloud life and victory over yourself as you embark on the journey of true transformation in Christ.

Through intentional reading and meditation on scripture, we are empowered to act justly, love mercy, and walk humbly with God (see Micah 6:8). The Holy Spirit endowed the believers of the early church with heavenly power to impact the world in such a way that has remained throughout generations. Our genuine and heartfelt prayer is that over the course of the next twenty-eight days, you will forge a newfound reliance on the Holy Spirit to inspire within you a desire to chart unprecedented waters in your relationship with the Lord, in order to effect the long-lasting change this world so desperately longs to see.

Day 1

Acts 1

Jesus instructed them, "Don't leave Jerusalem,
but wait here until you receive the gift I told you
about, the gift the Father has promised."
—Acts 1:4 (TPT)

The Wait

*L*iving in pursuit of God's promises requires learning how to navigate through seasons of waiting. The wait is the duration of time that lies between having received God's promise and the appointed time in which the promise is set to come to pass. In the waiting, God's promises can become buried beneath weariness, delay, and disappointment. In our seasons of waiting, it can be beneficial to consider what daily practices empowered the believers of the early church to wait on the Lord's promise of the Holy Spirit. With all diligence and the utmost intentionality, the believers of the early church chose to devote themselves to prayer, study of the word, and fellowship with God and with one another.

In the hustle and bustle of our fast-paced society, we must gently remind ourselves to revere and acknowledge the importance of patiently waiting on the Lord. The wait creates in us the endurance, character, and discipline needed to sustain the responsibility that comes with the promise. Devotion to prayer, study of the word, and fellowship with God and others prepares us for a life of submission in relation to the will of the Father. The pursuit of true intimacy with Jesus should remain our central priority, subsequently informing the layout of every other facet of our lives.

In their period of waiting, the disciples did not sit idly by. For forty days following Jesus's resurrection, they were active in their pursuit of more of Him, "learning about the things concerning the Kingdom of God."[1] We too must follow this pattern. Joined in fellowship and communion, we are to wait for what the Father has promised. Hebrews 10:25 urges that we do not forsake meeting together as believers. We

Norka Jenkins & Tayler Jenkins

are to show our love for God in our fellowship with Him and with one another. There is unprecedented power released unto us when we stand unified in agreement, waiting with great expectation for the Lord to deliver on what He promised. The place of fellowship is where the Lord waters the seed of His promise, cultivating and growing it until the fullness of its manifestation can be perceived in our reality.

Is there something you're believing God will provide today? Maybe it's been so long that you've given up hope. Continue to believe God is faithful and that He will deliver on the promise He has placed in your heart. Passive waiting can be detrimental to the fulfillment of what He has in store for you. Commit today to actively devote yourself to prayer and fellowship with God and godly community as you keep rooted and strengthened in Him in preparation to receive the fullness of His promise.

Reflection Questions

1. The scripture says that Jesus was sharing meals with the apostles when He instructed them to wait.[1] Likewise, your personal fellowship with Christ positions you to hear and to know His voice, and in your devotional time He will speak His promises and plans over your life. What are some of the promises Jesus has spoken to you?

2. As we wait on the promises of God to be fulfilled, we can sometimes experience discouragement. However, the early believers met together and were constantly united in prayer.[2] We are also instructed not to neglect our meeting together, so that we may encourage one another[3] and never stop praying.[4] In what ways have you stayed hopeful and expectant while waiting for God's promises to be fulfilled?

Father, I thank You for the promises You have spoken over me and that Your plans for me are good. Holy Spirit, while in the waiting, help me to never lose hope. I will stay in community with other believers where we can encourage and pray for one another in faith until Your plans are fulfilled in my life. As I study Your word, I thank You for leading me along the way. In Jesus's name, amen.

Day 2

Acts 2

Now when they heard this, they were cut to the heart
[with remorse and anxiety], and they said to Peter and the
rest of the Apostles, "Brothers, what are we to do?"
—Acts 2:37 (AMP)

The Promise of the Holy Spirit

At last, in successfully awaiting the promise of the Father, the apostles were divinely filled throughout their being with the Holy Spirit.[1] They were supplied with the supernatural ability to speak out clearly and appropriately concerning the hidden mysteries of God's kingdom. Are you aware that in the same manner, the Almighty One of heaven desires to supply you with the supernatural ability to effectively testify to His goodness and grace? Perhaps you feel a stirring on the inside, an awakening desire to experience more of Him and to bear the fruits and gifts of His Spirit. Peter led a crowd of three thousand to repentance in simply receiving what the Father had promised. He then urged new believers to receive the gift of the Holy Spirit for themselves. After hearing Peter's message, the people were troubled in their spirits and asked what they were to do.

Similarly, upon having repented of our sins and receiving Jesus as our Lord and Savior, our next steps must include seeking with all diligence the Holy Spirit to become effective ministers of the Father's glory and the grace offered us through His Son. The Holy Spirit is the only One who can lay bare what is in man's heart, convict him of his sin, and lead him to repentance. We must rely on the power of the Holy Spirit to fulfill the great commission on our lives as followers of Christ Jesus.

Whether you are a missionary in the field, a student in a university, pastor of a church, a working professional, or a stay-at-home parent, God has strategically positioned you for His divine purposes. Do

NORKA JENKINS & TAYLER JENKINS

not discredit the power of your witness. Rely on the Holy Spirit to tell of the goodness of God at every opportunity presented to you. Witnessing looks different for everyone, but the purpose remains one and the same. Do not be limited in your scope of how God can and even desires to use you. As Christ's ambassador, allow the Holy Spirit to minister through you as you testify on behalf of our God. Do not underestimate the power of your position. There is someone in your immediate circle of influence who needs what you have in the manner that only you can provide—and that is the message of faith, hope, and love found in Jesus.

Reflection Questions

1. The Holy Spirit is God's promise to those who believe in Christ Jesus.[2] When we receive the Holy Spirit, He distributes, activates, and operates different gifts in and through us.[3] How can you identify which spiritual gifts have been given to you?

2. God desires to use us where we are. Peter was a fisherman, and by the power of the Holy Spirit he was transformed to an apostle who boldly preached the message of the Messiah. How has your walk as a believer been transformed by the Holy Spirit?

Father, thank You for the promised gift of Your Holy Spirit. I declare by faith that I have received Your Holy Spirit in the name of Jesus. You alone have decided which spiritual gift each person should have. Help me to identify my specific gifts. Holy Spirit, thank You for the conviction that transforms my life into the image of Christ. I know You have strategically positioned me where I am, and I will testify of Your goodness at every opportunity. In Jesus's name, amen.

Day 3

Acts 3

But I'll give you what I have. In the name of Jesus
Christ, the Nazarene, get up and walk!

—Acts 3:6 (NLT)

I'll Give You What I Have

*I*n the case of the lame beggar, it was more than evident to all those passing by that his ailment was a physical one. Day after day, the beggar sat before the temple gates, seeking provision to supply for his financial needs. Walking according to the Spirit, the apostles Peter and John recognized the opportunity to provide for this man more than he ever realized could be attained for himself. It is crucial to recognize that the power and authority you have in Christ Jesus *is* the most valuable of all that you possess. See yourself in light of the apostles—that the power that flowed through them to administer healing to the beggar is the very same power that flows through you at the moment you receive the Holy Spirit. This power is not meant to be contained, but to be shared with others.

Overflowing with gratitude at being strengthened and healed in his physical body, the formerly lame beggar immediately began praising God, and all the people in the temple heard this. In their willingness to give generously of what they had, the apostles brought glory to the name of Jesus through the power of the Holy Spirit at work through them. The beggar was not only made perfect in health, but he received complete wholeness in his spirit.[1]

It is only by the power of God and the supernatural gifts of the Spirit that we have the ability to administer healing that reaches into the very depths of one's soul. The Amplified Bible defines spiritual gifts as special abilities given by the grace and extraordinary power of the Holy Spirit operating in believers.[2] As you look for opportunities to be generous, do not be limited by the scope of your finances, but also consider what spiritual gifts you have been endowed with in order to bless others (see 1 Corinthians 12). Seek wisdom from the Lord today in how you can give generously from *all* you have been given. The apostle Paul assures us that as we minister to others through our generosity, we will meet the needs of the believers, and they will joyfully express their thanks to God.[3]

Through your faith in the name of Jesus, you have been healed in every way one can achieve healing.[4] Use your spiritual gifts to bless and to refresh others, and the word of our God promises that you too will be refreshed.[5] Have faith and confidence in knowing that the Spirit of the Lord is upon you, and His power is already at work within you. When we surrender to the Lord what we have, we position ourselves to witness Him take what could never be enough in us and work a supernatural blessing that far exceeds our wildest imagination.[6]

Reflection Questions

1. Our generosity is not limited to our monetary resources. There are spiritual gifts given to us by the Holy Spirit so we can help one another.[7] By the power of the Holy Spirit, the gift of healing was administered through Peter. How are you currently using your gifts to help others?

2. Through the apostles's faith in the name of Jesus, the beggar not only received healing in his physical body, he received complete wholeness. All the people saw him walking and praising God, and they were filled with wonder and amazement.[8] When the needs of believers are met, joyful expressions of thanksgiving are given to God.[9] Describe how you are actively developing and refining your gifts to minister to others.

Father, I thank you for giving me spiritual gifts that are to be used to help others. Holy Spirit, thank you for revealing to me what my gifts are, and give me wisdom as to how I am to develop and utilize them for the kingdom of God. My spiritual gifts are not just for me, but they are to be used to meet the needs of those around me. Father, I will graciously give what I have so that your people may joyfully express their many thanksgivings to You. In Jesus's name, amen.

Day 4

Acts 4

But to keep them from spreading their
propaganda any further, we must warn them
not to speak to anyone in Jesus' name again.

—Acts 4:17 (NLT)

Extraordinary Boldness

*T*here is a special ability given to us by the Holy Spirit which enables us to speak the word of God regardless of our qualifications. Peter and John were ordinary men with no special training in the scriptures.[1] In spite of this reality, the religious leaders recognized the newly deemed apostles as men having been followers of Jesus. In light of your speech, conduct, and the way that you love others, is the world able to recognize that you are a follower of Christ?[2]

God uses the foolish things of this world to confound the wise.[3] He so graciously empties us of our credentials in order to display His mighty working power through us. "We are not qualified to do anything on our own, our qualifications come from God."[4] In His divine nature, God takes what is ordinary and chooses to reflect the hidden mysteries of the extraordinary. Maybe today you feel as though you lack the education, the experience, the special training, or even the resources to do the very thing God has called you to. Congratulations, you are uniquely qualified to share the message of Christ's gospel!

Through the inner workings of the Holy Spirit, we have been given great boldness and authority in Jesus's name to preach the word in the face of our adversaries. The spirit of intimidation seeks to refrain believers from proclaiming the name of Jesus for fear of offending an unbelieving world. However, where there exists the spirit of fear and intimidation, Christ has already given us a spirit of power, love, and a sound mind to triumph in victory.[5] The enemy sees Jesus in you, and his overwhelming desire is to silence your witness so that you fail to testify concerning the things of God. The apostles Peter and John, alongside other believers, prayed that God would grant them great boldness in preaching the word, stretch out His hand of healing power through them, and accompany their witness by signs and wonders in the name of His holy Son, Jesus.[6] Joining our faith together with other believers encourages us to continue on paths of righteousness amid fear and intimidation.

The Lord is more than willing to strengthen you in your weakness; all you need to do is ask of Him, and He will supply the strength you need. The Lord, with His miraculous power as support, *will* accompany the witness of your testimony of His existence, goodness, and mercy. Stand up to fear and intimidation, and ask the Lord to grant you supernatural boldness and authority to proclaim the matchless name of Jesus!

Reflection Questions

1. The Jewish high court saw that Peter and John were uneducated and untrained, ordinary men.[7] Society can sometimes make us feel inadequate about what qualifies us, but by the power of the Holy Spirit, we are given supernatural ability, and He qualifies us.[8] How does this revelation of truth shift your perspective of what qualifies you to minister?

2. There is power in agreement.[9] The church came together and prayed that the Lord grant them great confidence to declare the message of salvation, and they were all filled with the Holy Spirit and began to speak with boldness and courage.[10] Who in your community of believers can you come into agreement with and ask the Lord to grant you extraordinary boldness?

Father, in the name of Jesus, I thank You for using ordinary people to accomplish extraordinary things for Your kingdom. Being in the presence of Jesus qualifies me to do what You've called for me to do. I am not sufficiently qualified in myself, but my sufficiency and qualifications come from You. You have commanded me to be strong and courageous, so I pray against the spirit of fear and intimidation and I thank You that I have boldness and authority in the name of Jesus to preach Your word and testify to Your miracles in my life. In Jesus's name, amen.

Day 5

Acts 5

But if this movement is of God, you
won't be able to stop it.

—Acts 5:39a (TPT)

Nothing Can Stop You

*I*s there a dream that exists within your heart? Have you ever been overwhelmed by a desire to accomplish more? Just as in the case of the apostles, it may very well be that you have a God-inspired mission and purpose just waiting to be fully realized through you. The enemy of your destiny will tempt you into aborting infantile dreams through fear. The fears of failure and persecution seek to imprison us in our comfortability, robbing us entirely of God-authored dreams. Comfort has deceived believers into choosing an unfulfilled life as they go through the motions of religious activity. In neglecting the spiritual fulfillment that comes only by answering God's call, we can become weary with religion and begin to wonder, "What is this all for?"

We must rely on the eternal truths embedded in God's word to inform us how to boldly go after our dreams in spite of fear. In answering the call of God on their lives, the apostles were all, at one point or another, met with persecution. The Amplified Bible reveals that despite being arrested, imprisoned, and flogged, the apostles believed they had no other choice but to obey God.[1] In fact, they were actually "thrilled that God had considered them worthy to suffer disgrace for the name of Jesus."[2]

We too may have to endure our own unique form of suffering in choosing to follow after the dream God has conceived in our heart. Regardless of how suffering may manifest—through criticism, ostracism, financial loss, or some form of abuse—the Lord has commanded His people to "be strong and courageous,"[3] and He promises to never burden us with more than we can bear.[4] No matter the degree of resistance from the forces of darkness, the Lord will raise up a mighty standard to sustain us in our fight.[5] Be reminded that "these light afflictions are but for a moment, producing in us an eternal weight of glory."[6]

No matter what may come against you, nothing will be able to stop you in your pursuit of His plan and purpose. The Lord will crown your efforts with success as you stand strong in your convictions and walk in obedience to His will.[7] You do not have to live in bondage, paralyzed by the fear of what others may think; for reverential fear of the Lord delivers us from the fear of man. Be encouraged that God will not leave you to fulfill His call according to your own devices. In His faithfulness, He will daily supply you with the strength, creativity, and boldness you need to fulfill your dreams. Dare to get excited about what is in your heart, confident of this: "He who began the good work within you will continue His work until it is finally finished on the day when Jesus Christ returns."[8]

Reflection Questions

1. The apostles, after being filled with the Holy Spirit, were walking in their purpose.[9] Despite persecution, they rejoiced in having been considered worthy to suffer for the name of Jesus—for they found ultimate fulfillment in proclaiming the good news of the gospel.[10] Performing "religious activity" can leave us void of fulfillment if we are not walking in our purpose. What *activities* are you involved in that are leaving you unfulfilled and keeping you from the true plans God has for you?

2. When your plans are of God, and not of man, nothing will be able to stop you.[11] In our obedience to God's call, we are commanded not to walk in fear of what man might say or do to us. We have no other choice but to obey God rather than men.[12] What are some fears that are keeping you from answering God's call?

Father, I thank You for Your Holy Spirit, who gives me the desire and ability to obey You. Reveal to me if there are commitments or religious activity in my life that I have taken on in order to please man. Give me the courage to say no to religion and yes to You. I thank You for Your supernatural peace and protection when I face opposition because I know that what You have started in me, You are faithful to perfect until the day of Your return. In Jesus's name, amen.

Day 6

Acts 6

Stephen, who was a man full of grace and supernatural
power, performed many astonishing signs and wonders
and mighty miracles among the people.

—Acts 6:8 (TPT)

Commissioned for Your Position

*W*e celebrate the apostles of the early church for the mighty men of valor they were. Naturally, we are in awe of the many signs, miracles, and wonders the Holy Spirit performed through them. It is clear that they were supernaturally anointed to preach the gospel of Jesus Christ. Yet, in spite of the grandeur of their illustrious résumé, the apostles recognized there were limitations concerning their responsibilities in the ministry.

There was a great need among the early believers that not even the healing power of Peter's shadow could supply. The apostles acknowledged their need of a man who was honorable, full of the Holy Spirit and wisdom, to adhere to the holy responsibility of food distribution. We as believers often mistakenly believe that the most effective place to serve in ministry is in preaching to a crowd of three thousand, and when our audience is devoid of such numbers we can feel as though our place is insignificant in the grand scheme of the Lord's design. However, through the leadership of the apostles, the Lord was after a man of faith who would be devoted to serving in such a unique place in ministry.

Stephen, "who was known as a man full of faith and overflowing with the Holy Spirit," was hand-chosen for the ministry of serving.[1] Imagine if Stephen had lusted after the position of Peter or John. Imagine if he had become distracted in desperate pursuit of a position apart from the one he was called to. What would have become of the believers during that day who felt their need was being overlooked?

You have been commissioned by God for your unique place in ministry. To be a minister simply requires the selfless ability to attend to the needs of others. It can be easy to deem your position as hardly important or ineffective, yet in reviewing the accounts of Acts chapter 6, we can see the necessity for everyone to confidently assume their place in the body of Christ. Whether you are a parent, a pastor, a CEO of a major corporation, or an usher in your local church, you have been anointed and commissioned by the Almighty One of heaven for that place. Do not underestimate the vitality of your unique position, for it is there that only you have the power through Jesus to perform signs, miracles, and wonders.

Reflection Questions

1. The apostles understood they could not neglect their primary purpose for teaching the word of God. They needed to delegate the responsibility of serving tables and managing the distribution of food to someone else. What are some responsibilities you have taken on that have caused you to neglect God's primary call on your life?

2. Stephen and several others were chosen, dedicated, and commissioned for the task of food distribution.[2] Stephen, although not an apostle, was still effective in ministry in this position.[3] How can you identify with Stephen in recognizing the value of where God has uniquely positioned you?

Father, I thank You that You have called me to a specific place among Your body of believers. Holy Spirit, help me to recognize when I have taken on more than what I was meant to handle. I thank You that there is no position too small in Your kingdom. Just as Stephen was, in my position within the body of Christ I am full of faith, full of grace, and overflowing with the Holy Spirit. In Jesus's name, amen.

Day 7

Acts 7

He crumpled to his knees and shouted in a loud voice,
"Our Lord, don't hold this sin against them."

—Acts 7:60 (TPT)

For Your Enemies

*W*hat lies within the heart of an intercessor that would move him, in the face of persecution, to pray for his enemies? What degree of love is poured out from the throne room of heaven that cries out for mercy even in the face of injustice? In modeling the same public display of affection as that of Jesus on the cross, Stephen—faced with certain death—fell to his knees in worship and cried out loudly that the Lord would pardon the sin of his murderers.[1] In beholding the glory of the Lord, Stephen would never come to witness what this seed of a prayer would ultimately produce in the unrepentant heart of a man witnessing his death: Saul of Tarsus.

What is yet to become of your enemies through your intercession? Are you aware of the power you have to alter the trajectory of the lives of those sent to harm you? Saul of Tarsus, later to become the apostle Paul, helps us to see that even unto death, the Lord works "all things together for good to those who are called according to His purpose."[2] In the timeless essence of our God, His promise extends even to those who have yet to be called and to those who have transitioned into eternity.

Stephen's address to the council threw the religious leaders into a fit of rage, accusing him of blaspheming against God. Yet not a word spoken out of the mouth of Stephen was devoid of scriptural truth. It is clear to see that the hearts of the council were in fact hardened to truth, and in turn, resistant to the work of the Holy Spirit. Familiarity with the word of God does not equate to the intimate knowledge of the truth that is revealed through the Holy Spirit. Hate blinds the heart to truth, and therefore, God's truth cannot be spoken or received where there is an absence of love.

Imagine for a moment what would become of this world if we would love in action through intercessory prayer. God, in His infinite wisdom, used the last, seemingly tragic sentence in Stephen's book of life as the opening statement of the apostle Paul's story of redemption. Do not harden your heart to the Lord's call for you to pray for those who persecute you[3], for when you do, you honor the Lord's command to love in this way. This sort of love comes not by the might of human effort, but by the internal workings of the Holy Spirit. Trust in the Lord's ability to take the most awful circumstance and use it for the ultimate good of His kingdom. The Lord is faithful to His promises even unto death. Stephen never did live to see the mighty work of the Lord through Saul, but on account of his prayer, a notorious murderer was transformed into a mighty apostle of the Lord Jesus Christ.

Reflection Questions

1. "You stubborn people. You are heathen at heart and deaf to truth. Must you forever resist the Holy Spirit?"[4] We are commanded not to be unresponsive to the working and guidance of the Holy Spirit.[5] How can you discern if your heart has been hardened and if you are unable to recognize truth when it is being spoken?

2. Jesus said, "Receive the Holy Spirit. If you forgive anyone's sins, they are forgiven. If you do not forgive them, they are not forgiven."[6] Examine your heart and ask the Holy Spirit to reveal to you if you have unforgiveness towards someone that has hurt you. Forgive and pray for them right now.

Father, I thank You that You have given me Your Holy Spirit to fill my heart with Your love so that I can recognize Your truth when I hear it. In the name of Jesus, help me not to be unresponsive to the working and guidance of the Holy Spirit. I ask for forgiveness for ever rejecting the truth of Your word. Let not my heart be hardened. Empower me to pray for my enemies and for those that have hurt me with the same heart that Stephen prayed for Saul. In Jesus's name, amen.

Day 8

Acts 8

Phillip asked him, "Sir, do you
understand what you're reading?"
—Acts 8:30b (TPT)

Do You Understand?

he hidden mysteries of God's kingdom only come through true revelation by the power of the Holy Spirit. After being baptized in the name of the Lord Jesus, the believers of the early church were admonished to receive the Holy Spirit. In the case of Jesus Himself, immediately upon being baptized, "the Holy Spirit descended upon Him ...," empowering Him to carry out the will of the Father.[1] The Holy Spirit sought to operate through Phillip to bring revelation knowledge to the Ethiopian eunuch. Fellowship with believers who are filled with and walk according to the Holy Spirit can help assist us on our journey to understanding the things of God.

We come to know Jesus intimately through the Holy Spirit's illumination of God's word. Through reading and meditation on the scriptures, we can familiarize ourselves with the character and devices of the Holy Spirit in order to recognize Him when He moves. As often as He chooses to display the miraculous power of heaven through many signs, miracles, and wonders, the Holy Spirit will likewise operate, for example, through the simplicity of a kind stranger's words. "The Holy Spirit [spoke] to Phillip" in order to draw the Ethiopian eunuch to faith in Jesus.[2] In listening to the voice of the Holy Spirit, Phillip partnered with heaven to be used as a vessel to accomplish the work of the Lord.

Maybe today you resonate with the eunuch's position as you wrestle with confusion concerning the things of God. Do not allow your desire to know more of God become paralyzed by frustration or shame. Rather, ask the Holy Spirit to breathe life into God's word and provide you with understanding. Do not be limited in your scope of how He may decide to answer you. The Spirit of God works in both overt and subtle ways. Regardless of the method—through fiery tongues or a gentle whisper—the Holy Spirit will reveal Himself when you simply ask of Him. Just as you received Jesus at the moment of salvation, choose to receive the free gift of the Holy Spirit by faith. The Holy Spirit is key to leading a fruitful and Spirit-led life. Receive the Holy Spirit and then commit to follow after His lead, both fully and forever.

Reflection Questions

1. The Holy Spirit gives us insight and revelation to the scriptures. He teaches us all things and reminds us of everything God tells us: all we have to do is ask.[3] Have you asked the Holy Spirit to provide you with an understanding of the Bible? Describe why it is important to participate in regular Bible study with other Spirit-filled believers.

2. God speaks to us through His word, and our relationship with Him is enriched daily as we get to know more about who He is and His will for our lives. He knows everything about each of us. How can you personally come to know more about Jesus?

Father, I thank You that I am filled with Your Holy Spirit and that He leads me into wisdom and truth in the knowledge and understanding of Your word. Your word is alive and powerful. It is sharper than the sharpest two-edged sword cutting between soul and spirit. Help me live on every word and meditate on it day and night, so that I can be transformed into the image of your son. In Jesus's name, amen.

Day 9

Acts 9

Isn't this the Saul who furiously persecuted those in
Jerusalem who called on the name of Jesus?

—Acts 9:21 (TPT)

A Radical Change

*A*t the moment we decide to believe in Jesus as our Lord and Savior and are filled with the Holy Spirit, He supernaturally works in us to be conformed into His image and likeness. Perhaps the Lord showcases no greater display of His transformative power than through the life of His chosen servant Saul. Within an hour of having been baptized and filled with the Holy Spirit, Saul—a man once full of "angry threats and rage" against the disciples of the Lord Jesus—could be found "in the synagogues preaching" that Jesus was the anointed Messiah.[1] The believers were astonished that this man who had once carried out much persecution against them was now being used as the Lord's messenger of the gospel. The radical transformation Saul had undergone was quite extraordinary.

Similarly, when we encounter Christ, there should be a distinct, identifiable difference in us that separates us from our old selves. Truly the apostle Paul was writing from a place of personal experience when he professed that, "If anyone is in Christ, he is a new creation."[2] Saul's encounter with Jesus dramatically altered the trajectory of not only his life, but also the life of the Church. Saul's conversion marked the beginning of a season of peace in which believers had the opportunity to grow together in their walk with the Lord.[3] One man's coming to Christ was revolutionary for believers in the grand scheme of eternity. The apostle Paul's decision to live as a prisoner for Christ[4] not only blessed the believers of his day, but has continued to bless believers presently and those who will believe in the generations to come.

What could become of your decision to live a life of undivided devotion to Christ? The sacrifice of one brought salvation to the entire world.[5] The transformation of one brought peace upon the body of Christ in a season of fear and uncertainty.[6] Countless examples of the one impacting the many are provided throughout scripture, and the principles are transferable to your own life. Regardless of your past mistakes and failures, the Lord desires to use you for His unique purpose and plan. Do not discount the Lord's ability to take what was intended for harm and destruction and use it for the ultimate good and growth of His Church. Our God is still in the business of producing radical change. Commit today to allowing the Lord to produce a radical change *in* you, then watch and see what He is able to accomplish *through* you.

Reflection Questions

1. Romans 8:29 says that God predestined us to be conformed to the image of Jesus, that He might be the firstborn among many brothers and sisters. We can be mirrors that brightly reflect the glory of the Lord.[7] Identify if there are any areas in your life that don't conform to the image of Jesus, and ask the Holy Spirit for a radical change.

2. When we come to believe in Jesus and are filled with the Holy Spirit, our lives should be transformed in such a way that it impacts those around us. The change in us has a direct influence on others. How has your transformation in Christ stirred up others to attain salvation?[8]

Father, thank You for the transforming power of Your Holy Spirit. I thank You that I am a new creation in Christ. The old has passed away, and all things are becoming new. Holy Spirit, use me to make a difference in the lives of those around me and radically change my life in such a way that others are stirred to seek the truth and be saved. In Jesus's name, amen.

Day 10

Acts 10

It makes no difference what race of people one belongs to.
If they show deep reverence for God, and are committed
to doing what's right, they are acceptable before Him.

—Acts 10:35 (TPT)

It Makes No Difference

*W*hy do you believe what you believe? What is your basis for such beliefs? 1 John 4 urges us to "test every spirit to see whether they are from God," so that we are able to discern the spirit of truth from the spirit of error.[1] Prior to any attempt at the demolition of divisive ideologies that would hinder the spread of the gospel, the Lord had to deal with Peter's attitude toward the Gentiles. The Lord revealed to Peter that nothing that He has declared to be clean can be rendered as unclean.[2] According to the new covenant, irrevocably sealed by the blood of Jesus, it makes no difference what race or culture you identify with. First and foremost, you belong to the Lord, and He has called you clean. Through Jesus, you possess every right under the laws of heaven and earth to be received into His kingdom as a child of God.

Peter's reservations seemed legitimate and justifiable, as they were rooted in the traditional customs of his culture. Yet, when we come to Christ, we know we must "put off [our] old [selves] … and put on the new self, created to be like God in true righteousness and holiness."[3] Oftentimes, bias will mask itself as religious pride and righteousness, when in truth it is a tactic of the enemy to delay Christ's desire for unity amongst His body. In order to obey God's directive to visit the Roman centurion and ultimately win him to Christ, Peter had to lay aside his old way of thinking and experience renewal in his mind regarding the Gentile's newly purchased place in the kingdom of God.

We must be willing to submit ourselves to the Lord in order to undergo a complete transformation in the renewing of our minds to war against the deception of the enemy. We must beware of sinful thoughts and attitudes that promote racial and cultural divisions among believers and submit to the Lord's desire for unity. As was revealed to Peter, we are never to regard anyone as being inferior, but we are to treat everyone on the same basis.[4] The message of hope, peace, and reconciliation through Jesus is offered to *everyone*. Deep reverence for God and a commitment to doing what is right is all that the Lord desires from those who identify as His servants.

Let us do away with the obstacles we have erected to keep people from the love of the Father. Test every spirit to see that they are indeed from God, ensuring that every belief and ideology you possess is wholly and firmly rooted in Him.

Reflection Questions

1. It was against their laws for the Jews to associate with Gentiles. However, the Holy Spirit instructed Peter to go to the home of Cornelius to share the message of Jesus Christ. Have you ever hesitated to share the gospel with someone because of their race or culture?

2. The spirit of hate and division that seeks to divide people on the basis of race and culture is not of God. We are commanded to love our neighbors,[5] and hate in our heart is like murder in the eyes of Jesus.[6] Ask the Holy Spirit for revelation of any prejudices in your heart that cause divisions within the body of Christ.

Father, I thank You in the name of Jesus for giving me revelation of the truth of Your word today—that You view no one as inferior. We were all created in Your image; therefore, I will not judge anyone. Your word says it makes no difference what race of people one belongs to. If they show deep reverence for You and are committed to doing what's right, they are acceptable before You. Holy Spirit, I ask You to renew my mind and remove any prejudices in my heart that have caused divisions instead of unity in the church. Thank You for removing any biases that would hinder me from sharing Your gospel with others. In Jesus's name, amen.

Day 11

Acts 11

He encouraged the believers to remain faithful and
to cling to the Lord with passionate hearts.

—Acts 11:23b (TPT)

Seasons of Hardship

*I*n the adverse seasons of life, it is critical to remain faithful in fellowship with the Lord. Through trials and tribulations, the word of God and the life-giving power of the Holy Spirit provide sustenance. Regular reading and meditation on scripture alongside communing with other believers anchors our hearts to the unchanging character of God, producing hope in us for the promised joy to come.[1]

Beware of perpetual isolation, which diminishes the ability of the Lord and others to minister hope to your hurting spirit. The Lord honored the faithfulness of His church as they continued coming together to proclaim the message of salvation through Jesus despite recently having exited a period of rampant persecution. "The mighty power of the Lord was with them" in their determination to cling to Him with passionate hearts.[2] Determine for yourself today that no matter the season, you will remain connected to the Lord as your source of strength.

Intensified through suffering, the Lord desires to use you as His conduit through which He can provide for the needs of His kingdom. The Holy Spirit communicated to the prophet Agabus a rising need in the body of Christ as a result of the coming famine. In his availability to the Lord, Agabus was able to partner with other believers and prepare for the opportunity to "send relief to [the believers] living in Judea."[3] The cries of the Lord's people have not fallen on deaf ears. Rather, the Holy Spirit is working at all times to fulfill His longing of meeting the needs of His people through us.

In our moment of need, it can be difficult to identify what we have to give away to others for fear of not having enough for ourselves.

Norka Jenkins & Tayler Jenkins

Rest in knowing that when you give according to your ability, the Lord will liberally supply your every need.[4] God has supplied you with everything you need to be a blessing to others. Consider your resources, time, and talents when seeking the Holy Spirit for wisdom concerning what you have to give. Entrust every gift of yours to the Lord, and wait with great expectation for the abundant harvest He is sure to produce in the lives of those He reaches through your generosity. Remaining faithful and diligent to the call of the Lord is critical when it is dark in your life and you are waiting for the dawn to break. Cling to the Lord in determination through trying times, believing in faith that His mighty hand is working to see you through.

Reflection Questions

1. Our journey of faith was never meant to be walked out in isolation. The Holy Spirit gives us the ability to remain strong and faithful in Jesus through community. It is important for us to share with other believers about the goodness and faithfulness of God. How are you encouraging others, with an unwavering heart, to stay true and devoted to the Lord in difficult seasons?[5]

2. When we give of our resources, time, and talents, God makes provision for our spiritual and material needs. Proverbs 11:25 says that the "generous will prosper; those who refresh others will themselves be refreshed." Describe practical ways you can be of service to other believers during your times of hardship.

Father, I thank You for my local church and for the understanding of the importance of fellowship with other believers. Thank You for the gift of generosity and the opportunity to provide for the needs of Your people during their times of hardship and my own. Holy Spirit, help me to continue in fellowship and to remain faithful to Your voice in every season. In Jesus's name, amen.

Day 12

Acts 12

The church went into a season of intense
intercession, asking God to free him.

—Acts 12:5 (TPT)

Never Stop Praying

*I*ntercession is defined as the act of interceding or intervening on someone's behalf. Maybe your image of an intercessor extends only to your fiery, Holy-Spirit filled grandmother or perhaps the prayer partners at your church. In truth, spiritual intercession is simply the act of offering a prayer on behalf of another person. Peter was caught in the midst of intense spiritual warfare as King Herod enacted persecution against the church. Rather than be paralyzed with fear, the church rose up in power to engage in a period of intense and fervent prayer on Peter's behalf. It is critical to note that yet while they were still praying, an angel of the Lord appeared before Peter and "rescued [him] from the clutches of Herod and from what the Jewish leaders had planned."[1]

The body of Christ united in prayer moves the hand of God. As in the upper room, the Spirit of the Lord will be in their midst, accompanied by deliverance and power. The believers—and even Peter himself initially—were in disbelief at the Lord's miraculous display of power in answer to their prayer.[2] Their response begs the question, "Well, what did they expect?" When you pray, what do *you* expect? What inspires you to pray? Being intentional in our prayer life empowers us to stand firm against the enemy and bind powers and principalities that would seek to inhibit the work of God in our communities and in our lives. It can be difficult to envision ourselves as prayer warriors or intercessors. Paul in Ephesians 6:18 instructs us to "pray at all times and on every occasion [and to] stay alert and be persistent in ... prayer for all believers everywhere." The fact of the matter is, the Lord has called us to be a praying church, and we should not shy away from this call. It is through intercessory prayer that God partners with humanity in seeing His kingdom come and His will be done on earth as it is in heaven.[3]

Upon arriving at the house of Mary, mother of John and Mark, Peter was sure to share with them "the miraculous way the Lord brought him out of prison."[4] Sometimes, we fail to tell others of the work the Lord has done in our lives, because we want to appear humble and not flaunt our victories before those who are going through seasons of hardship. However, we must realize that the purpose of a praise report is to serve as encouragement for other believers to continue on in prayer. You give the Lord the glory due His name when you remember to tell others of what He has done.

Perhaps you have shied away from intercession for fear of engaging in intense spiritual warfare; be reminded that the Lord has armed you with strength for every battle.[5] Unleash the power of the Holy Spirit to work in your situation and the situation of others through your intercession. Declare in faith, believing and not doubting, that the Spirit of the Lord is moving on your behalf.

Reflection Questions

1. 1 Thessalonians 5:17 instructs us simply to "never stop praying"; however, we have an adversary that wants us to stop. We have all been asked to pray for someone, but on occasion have forgotten to pray for them. How are you remaining persistent in prayer so that the miracles of God are not hindered in your life and in the lives of others?

2. Peter told the believers to let the others know the miraculous way the Lord brought him out of prison. When we receive an answer to prayer, it is critical that we share what God has done. It is our testimony that stirs up the faith of other believers and encourages them to keep praying. What are some of the answered prayers you've recently received? Have you shared God's faithfulness with someone today?

Father, I thank You that You are forever the same yesterday, today and tomorrow. You are still performing miracles, even right now. You have called for me to pray in the Spirit at all times and on every occasion—to be alert and persistent in my prayers for all believers everywhere. Holy Spirit, recall to my remembrance those You would have for me to intercede for and help me to never stop praying. I believe Your angels are working in this very moment in their life and in mine. In Jesus's name, amen.

Day 13

Acts 13

Paul stared into his eyes and rebuked him.

—Acts 13:9 (TPT)

Rebuke Them Sharply

here is a negative stigma surrounding a kingdom principle necessary for continued growth and edification in Christ Jesus: rebuke. Rebuke is a device of the Holy Spirit purposed to preserve the integrity of God's truth and God's church. We see this demonstrated in the case of Paul and Barnabas in their encounter with a sorcerer and false prophet, Elymas. Elymas "also went by the name of 'son of Jesus'," yet it was strikingly evident that his intent was "to prevent the governor from believing" the message of the gospel.[1] When on assignment for the Lord, we will encounter forces of darkness that seek to inhibit the work of the Holy Spirit through us. It is critical that we not only identify such spirits through the use of our discernment, but that we stand up to such spirits in the boldness and authority given us in Christ Jesus.

Fear of persecution, confrontation, or even rejection from our peers can cause us to shy away from the need to rebuke spirits that seek to "pervert ... the truth of God into lies."[2] These spirits are not shy in their attempt to usurp the power of the church through the corruption of truth; neither should we be timid in exercising our God-given authority in Christ over such spirits. We must continually be washed by the cleansing of God's word in order to effectively war against the tactics and schemes of the enemy. We must not limit the possibility of error to extend only to a fallen and sinful world, but to be mindful of the enemy's subtle and continual grasping at the church.

The spirit of religion is equally a demonic force seeking to disrupt the work of the Holy Spirit *inside* of the church, a force that is in desperate need of rebuke. The spirit of religion is hypocritical, mean, and judgmental in nature. The spirit thrives off gossip, murmur, and slander against fellow congregants and leaders in the church. Devoid of love, the spirit of religion adopts a pharisaical attitude and undermines the message of hope and redemption in Christ. A true and genuine relationship with Jesus as our Lord and Savior must be pursued over the adoption of a religious attitude in which we are blind to our own faults and defects.

There is a delicate balance we as believers must maintain in order to truly walk in the same manner of love and truth as our Lord Jesus Christ. In order to achieve such a feat, we must rely exclusively on the Holy Spirit. Following His internal promptings, the Spirit of Truth will lead us and "guide [us] into all truth."[3] Be in constant search for pride, selfishness, and judgmental attitudes that try to attach themselves to your heart. Familiarize yourself with the word of God in order to discern the Spirit of Truth from the spirit of lies and deceits. When you recognize a spirit that is working against the truth and knowledge of Christ, be bold in binding such spirits. The Holy Spirit gives us the power and boldness to speak truth into any situation. Do not allow adversarial spirits cause you to back down in timidity and fear. You have been anointed for a special work. Move forward in boldness, truth, and love.

Reflection Questions

1. Religion is not the same as having a relationship with Jesus Christ. Through our relationship with Jesus, the Holy Spirit is our advocate, and the spirit of religion is our adversary. Religion can be jealous; it contradicts and opposes the things of God. In what ways can you guard yourself against the snares of religion?

2. John 16:13 says that when the Spirit of Truth has come, He will guide you into all truth. Paul recognized that the sorcerer was perverting the true ways of the Lord, and being filled with the Holy Spirit, spoke a stern rebuke to him. Describe a time when you were given correction and it led you back to living a life of truth in keeping with the word of God.

Father, I thank You for Your Holy Spirit guiding me into all knowledge of truth. I thank You for helping me to discern those things which are contrary to Your word and for giving me the courage and boldness to always speak Your truth with confidence and in love. Holy Spirit, deliver me from any form of religion, and position my heart to receive sharp correction so that I can be strong in faith and free from doctrinal error. In Jesus's name, amen

Day 14

Acts 14

Paul discerned that this man had faith
in his heart to be healed.

—Acts 14:9 (TPT)

What Do You Expect?

*D*o you have hope for the possibility of things not yet seen? Our level of faith pulls the kingdom of God from the unseen realm into reality. If our desire is to experience and showcase displays of God's heavenly, miraculous glory as the apostles did here on earth, we must position ourselves to receive from God in faith.

In Acts 14:9, Paul ministered healing to a man who had the faith to believe in what he had never seen. Through his eyes of faith, this man saw the possibility of a reality unbeknownst to him, in which he was healed of his infirmity. Similar to the story of the woman with the issue of blood in Luke 8, the crippled man's faith truly made him whole.[1] The Holy Spirit desires to make a great display of power through your life—not for your glory, but for the glory of the Father. This is demonstrated through Jesus raising Lazarus from the dead. Through this miraculous display of power, Jesus taught that our belief in God would result in seeing the glory of God revealed.[2]

Our faith in God and expectation to see Him move in our life brings honor to Him before an unbelieving world. Be honest in your assessment of the level of faith you have placed in God. Is your perception of God's power limited to His sovereignty, or do you believe in His providence as well? God is a good Father who desires to take care of His children. However, God is a gentleman and will not force His hand upon you. We must invite God through our faith to become intimately involved in every aspect of our lives. In doing so, we have the opportunity to foster a growing relationship with God in getting to experience *all* of who He truly is. Tried, true, and mature faith in God extends beyond lip service and believes in every dimension of being that the kingdom of God is *living* by God's power.[3] You do not have to lower your expectations of God in order to spare yourself the potential of disappointment. God is not a man that He should lie[4], and when you relinquish control of your plans to Him, He will exceed your every expectation.[5]

Our responsibility of faith extends beyond the scope of our lives and helps to bring deliverance and healing to those in need. Paul discerned in his spirit the faith of a man expecting to be healed and acted accordingly. The Holy Spirit has given you supernatural ability to believe on behalf of others and prophesy deliverance and victory into their lives as "clear evidence of [God's] goodness."[6] Increase your level of expectation in the Lord in order to experience Him for *all* of Who He is and receive in faith the miracles He longs to perform through you in order to reveal His glory.

Reflection Questions

1. Hebrews 11:1 tells us that faith is the substance of things hoped for, the evidence of things not seen, and Jesus said that if we would believe, we would see the glory of God. Paul saw that the crippled man had faith in his heart to be healed; Paul commanded him to stand to his feet, and he walked. What do you have faith for, and are you able to discern when someone else is in need of a miraculous spiritual or physical healing?

2. Our life should also reflect clear evidence of God's goodness. Jesus waited four days before raising Lazarus from the dead, so that those standing by would believe that the Father had sent him.[7] What evidence of God's power do others see in your life that can be used to draw them to Jesus?

Father, I thank You that Your Holy Spirit has given me discernment to see when others are in need of healing from you. Strengthen my faith so that I will always have an expectation for you to perform miracles and never lose hope for what you can do in my life and in the lives of those around me. Your word says that the kingdom of God is not just a lot of talk; it's living by your power. So, Holy Spirit, I ask that my life may always demonstrate and reflect the power of God until it overflows. In Jesus's name, amen.

Day 15

Acts 15

So why on earth would you limit God's grace by placing
a yoke of religious duties on the shoulders of believers
that neither we nor our ancestors were able to bear?
—Acts 15:10 (TPT)

By Grace Alone

*G*od's free gift of grace empowers us to walk in true freedom from sin and the burden of the law. The apostles Paul, Barnabas, Peter, and James, on separate occasions, spoke out against the attempts of false teachers and converts from the sect of the Pharisees to impose upon the non-Jewish believers the keeping of the law of Moses as a requirement for salvation.[1]

Our earthly mentality suggests that God's love and acceptance of us is contingent upon our performance. In striving, we hinder our ability to come into agreement with the truth regarding salvation— that it is a *free gift* we receive through faith in Jesus Christ. Do not limit the work of grace in your life in trying to assume the place of Jesus as Lord and Savior. Surrender to the power of grace. In submission to the work of the Holy Spirit through grace, we are empowered to do what cannot be done in the natural.

Shame, guilt, and condemnation as a result of sin are inhibitors on our journey to receiving God's grace. However, we have been commanded to "stand firm" and not let ourselves be "burdened again by a yoke of slavery."[2] Grace alone is what the Lord offers us in order to achieve freedom from those things that seek to keep us in bondage. In receiving the Lord's grace for yourself, you are uniquely positioned to extend grace to others. Do not posture as a stumbling block for other believers on their way to establishing a relationship with the Lord by enforcing traditional practices as stipulations for salvation. The basis for our salvation is that we have

NORKA JENKINS & TAYLER JENKINS

been freely given what could never be earned. Our need of grace goes beyond our moment of salvation and extends into every area of our walk. Lean into grace, for it is by grace alone we can truly be changed.

Reflection Questions

1. Upon receiving the free gift of salvation, we can sometimes fall into performance-based Christianity, only to find ourselves frustrated. If we seek to be justified through the law, we have fallen from grace.[3] Are you able to identify when you are living by grace or operating in your own ability?

2. "It is not as a result of [our] works or [our] attempts to keep the law, so that [we will not] be able to boast or take credit for [our] salvation."[4] In stark contrast to this verse, the religious leaders were trying to impose the law on the non-Jewish believers. Do you find yourself hindering the spiritual growth of other believers by imposing religious duties and traditions, or do you allow the Holy Spirit to extend grace to others through you?

Father, Your word says that You resist the proud, but You provide grace to the humble. I thank You for unmerited favor (grace) and for the strength and power given to me by Your Holy Spirit for salvation. I understand that I am not justified by my works, but only by grace through faith. Your grace is more than enough. Holy Spirit, help me to extend and receive the free gift of grace daily. In Jesus's name, amen.

Day 16

Acts 16

Paul and Silas, undaunted, prayed in the middle of
the night and sang songs of praise to God, while all
the other prisoners listened to their worship.

—Acts 16:25 (TPT)

Undaunted

As believers in Christ, we will inevitably experience opposition in our walk. If we fail to interpret periods of suffering and understand their divine purpose, we can begin to question the goodness and faithfulness of God. While on mission for the Lord, a demonic spirit taunted the apostles until Paul, being "greatly annoyed *and* worn out," exercised his authority in Christ and commanded the spirit to come out of the young slave girl.[1] When mercilessly thrown into prison, rather than being overtaken by feelings of fear and self-pity, Paul and Silas "prayed in the middle of the night and sang songs of praises to God."[2] Though bound and imprisoned in the natural, Paul and Silas experienced a supernatural freedom that left them undaunted in the face of suffering.

Though sometimes hard to muster while in the throes of struggle, praise has the power to rejuvenate a depleted spirit. In offering praises to God, Paul and Silas released the power of the Holy Spirit to orchestrate freedom on their behalf. An earthquake "shook the foundations of the prison," and deliverance found them all at once.[3] It may be at times hard to believe, but God has a plan and a purpose that is proven good through such fiery trials. Through what he suffered, Paul was empowered in his understanding that "suffering produces perseverance; perseverance, character; and character, hope. And hope does not put us to shame, because God's love has been poured out into our hearts through the Holy Spirit, who has been given to us."[4] Exercise your authority in Christ over principalities that seek to render you powerless in your walk during times of suffering. Sing praises to the Lord, prophesying the victory that is sure to come in your life.

Finally, dare to believe that God not only can, but is more than willing to give you beauty for your ashes.[5]

God used for His glory what was intended for harm in winning the jailer and his entire household to Himself through what the apostles suffered. Had Paul and Silas never been thrown in jail, the jailer would have never experienced the joy of a life spent in devotion to Jesus. In the midst of a difficult season, your decision to praise God holds the greatest potential for inspiring others to endure. The enemy desires nothing more than to disrupt the work of the Lord in your life. Be encouraged today that the God of the universe is for you, and He will never leave you to your own devices against the enemy of the age. Run to Him when it is darkest in your life, and trust that He will restore joy back to you. The work of the Lord continues until the return of Christ Jesus, and in the end, it will all work together for your highest good.[6]

Reflection Questions

1. Demonic opposition will come when we are on mission for Christ. Immediately after Paul spoke by his authority in Jesus to the demon, both he and Silas were severely beaten and thrown into prison. While on mission for God, how have you been derailed by danger, difficulty, or disappointment?

2. Supernatural power exists in our prayer, praise, and worship to God, and we are to keep on rejoicing as we share in Christ's sufferings.[7] His pattern for our freedom and deliverance is revealed in Acts 16. How do you respond when you are faced with opposition?

Father, Your word says that tests and trials come to make us stronger. Holy Spirit, give me strength and encourage me when I am faced with danger, difficulty, or disappointment. Father, You are enthroned upon the praises of Your people, and when I cry out to You because I trust You, You said that You will rescue me and deliver me. Thank You. Because I can depend on You, I will never be disappointed or ashamed. In Jesus's name, amen.

Day 17

Acts 17

It is through Him that we live and
function and have our identity.

—Acts 17:28 (TPT)

I Found Him

$\mathcal{M}$ ankind offering their worship to man-made images is a phenomenon dating back to the beginning of creation. Paul sought to eradicate such behaviors in his address to the leaders of Athens. In observance of their "extravagant … worship of idols," Paul seized the opportunity to introduce the Athenians to the "Unknown God."[1] The traditional worship of idols has subtly taken on various new forms in our day and age. Our man-made images of today mask themselves in the form of entertainment, our perceptions of other people, a position or title, and the relationships we keep or seek. While each category is not innately sinful in and of itself, anything left unsubmitted to God holds the potential for becoming an idol. The Athenians, in their worship of many idols, sought to satisfy their desire for knowledge and understanding of "rather strange things."[2]

Presently, we have erected idols to satiate almost every desire we possess. God has placed in us desires impossible to be satisfied apart from Him, with hopes that one day, in our desperate longing, we would "feel [our] way to Him and find Him."[3] Were you aware that the Lord our God has desires too and that He has made us, as extensions of Himself, deeply and intimately aware of such desires through His Holy Spirit, alive in us? Revealed in the once-hidden mysteries of His word, the Lord is whispering to us, "And once you have searched for me and found me with all your heart, hold onto me and don't let me go."[4] Even a seemingly idyllic image of the Creator could not satisfy our soul's need of who He *truly* is. Allow the romantic reality and truth of God to shatter the need of worthless idols. Allow everything—from your identity to your soul's deepest desires—to become firmly rooted and established in Christ, so that you may be "strengthened in the faith ... and overflowing with thankfulness."[5] God desires for you to live a life of complete joy and satisfaction in Him alone. Our God is a jealous God, which is why we have been encouraged to live a life of "undivided devotion to [Him]."[6]

Your desire for relationship and recognition was placed in you by God as motivation to seek Him. Feeble attempts at suppressing such desires in order to fulfill false religious obligations can result in self-reprimand, general feelings of resentment, an overpowering sense of hopelessness, and depression. You were made to want *Him*; lean into this truth and cease running from it. Free this world and everything in it of the burden to supply what it never was intended to. In Him, all is found, and when you find Him, hold fast and never let go.

Reflection Questions

1. The One who created us in His image satisfies everything that we could ever want or need. His purpose is for us to feel our way toward him and find him, and when we find him, we find our identity in Him. Our identity is not found in our relationships apart from Jesus, nor are they found in our positions, titles, or ambitions. Ask the Holy Spirit to reveal to you and describe the truth of who you are in Christ.

2. 1 Corinthians 7:35 says that we should do whatever will help us to serve the Lord best, with as few distractions as possible. However, we look to other things and deny that God is enough for us. God says that we should not have any other gods before Him, because He is a jealous God. What are some of the idols in your life that come before God?

Father, I thank You that I am fearsomely and wonderfully made, and my frame was not hidden from You when you made me in secret. In You, I live and move and exist, and I am Your offspring. Holy Spirit, I ask that You remind me every day of who I am in Christ Jesus and help me to remove my man-made idols that would distract me from living a life of undivided devotion to You. I submit them all to You, for I have found the One whom my soul loves, and I will not let You go. In Jesus's name, amen.

Day 18

Acts 18

Because I am with you. No one will be able to hurt you.

—Acts 18:10 (TPT)

Don't Ever Be Afraid

Throughout scripture, the Lord commands us to be courageous and to trust Him. Paul could have given in to fear and discouragement after being "viciously slandered" and "abuse[d]" by his Jewish counterparts.[1] However, upon receiving an encouraging word through a vision from the Holy Spirit, Paul was granted the staying power to remain faithfully committed to the place and people he was called to serve.[2]

Fear and discouragement are tactics the enemy uses to steer you away from the call of God on your life. A word of encouragement from the Lord is critical to overcoming such feelings. The words the Lord spoke to Paul parallel those He once spoke to His servant Joshua when leading the Israelites into their Promised Land: "This is my command—be strong and courageous! Do not be afraid or discouraged. For the Lord your God is with you wherever you go."[3] The promises of God echoed throughout scripture are the same words He is speaking to you and me today. God offers us eternal peace, comfort, and protection found in His word, and through His Holy Spirit, He empowers us to "press toward the mark for the prize of the high calling of God in Christ Jesus."[4]

You have been given a spirit of power to stand before whatever makes you feel afraid. Command fear to bow in submission to the Lord Jesus, and step into your calling. In spite of what Paul may have faced, the Lord promised him that nothing would be able to hurt him while he carried out his ministry of the gospel in Macedonia.[5] The Lord's promise of protection sustained Paul in moments when he may have been tempted to give up in fear. Though you may *feel* afraid, you do not have to remain prisoner to it, paralyzed by its grip. Recall the Garden of Gethsemane, just moments prior to Jesus's arrest. Deeply distressed and troubled, Jesus fell flat on His face in prayer to God the Father, seeking the strength and faith He would need to endure His greatest trial.[6] The glorious truth revealed through the life, death, and resurrection of Jesus is that He so willingly identified with us and our humanity. Through what He suffered, Jesus has given us the right to stand boldly before those things that would seek to intimidate or discourage us and secure our victory in His name.

When considering giving up and moving on, first determine if that is the Lord's will for you or if He intends to develop in you a strength that comes only by the staying power of His Holy Spirit. Determine in your heart to stand up to fear and seek the Lord for the courage required to carry out His will.

Reflection Questions

1. Jesus knows that our fears can lead us into discouragement and hopelessness. Paul faced opposition and insults while teaching the word of God, but the Lord spoke to Paul in a vision and told him to never be afraid or intimidated. Can you recall a time when you were overcome with fear, but the Holy Spirit encouraged you to stay the course?

2. Paul was given the word that no one would be able to hurt him because there were still many for him to reach that the Lord had called. By the power of His Holy Spirit, God provides us with supernatural protection through whatever He has purposed us to do. Describe a time when you experienced God's supernatural protection while performing His work.

Father, I thank You that You have repeatedly commanded us in Your word to never be afraid. You have not given me a spirit of fear and timidity, but of power, of love, and a sound mind. I thank You that the good work You have started within me will continue until it is finished. I thank You for Your Holy Spirit that has been sent to encourage me, comfort me, and protect me when I face opposition in carrying out Your will for my life. Thank You, Father, for Your promise to never leave me nor forsake me. In Jesus's name, amen.

Day 19

Acts 19

I know Jesus, and I know Paul, but who are you?

—Acts 19:15 (NLT)

Identity

"Who are you?"[1] This seemingly innocuous question propelled many Jews and non-Jews of Ephesus toward repentance and faith in Christ. As people were drawn to the light of salvation in Jesus, "large numbers of those ... practicing magic took all of their books and scrolls of spells and incantations and publicly burned them"—their actions unhindered by the fact that their precious works were worth several millions of dollars.[2] In this public denunciation of their former lives, "the name of the Lord Jesus was greatly honored."[3] The believers in Ephesus now revered their identity in Christ as their most valuable asset.

Far less accepting of the shift in religious ideology in Ephesus were a silversmith named Demetrius and the various tradespeople whose prosperous livelihood was dependent upon the Ephesians worship of the goddess Artemis.[4] Fear of losing out on their source of wealth inhibited Demetrius and the tradespeople from placing their identity, faith, and trust in Jesus.

Similarly, rather than place our trust in Christ as the source of everything we need, we can mistakenly rely on our occupation or possessions to provide us with the security and/or sense of identity we long for.

Jesus teaches us to "seek first His kingdom and His righteousness," and all we need will be given to us as well.[5] As a result of seeking righteousness, the word of God reveals that "life, prosperity, and honor" follow suit.[6] This truth is revealed in the life of King Solomon, who, in genuine pursuit after the wisdom of God, was promised long life, prosperity, and honor from the Lord Himself.[7] To rearrange the

NORKA JENKINS & TAYLER JENKINS

Lord's order and pursue life, prosperity, and honor before pursuing His kingdom is error and does not inspire the Lord's true blessing. Solemn fear of the Lord is the beginning of knowledge—including the knowledge of who you are in Him.[8]

We are powerless if we fail to identify with Jesus. Rather than be identified according to your occupation or material possessions, allow your identity in Christ to impact your place of work, and look for opportunities to minister to the needs of those you have been uniquely positioned to influence. The message of Jesus is worth more than any possession, and who you are in Him is more noteworthy than any job title. In whatever you do, seek to glorify God through it. Your identity in Christ *is* your most valuable asset and attribute. Search the word of God, and awaken to the revelation of who you are in Him.

Reflection Questions

1. Many of the believers who were practicing magic publicly confessed their sin and burned their incantation books, which were of significant value. Once we have identified who we are in Christ, we also come to know him as the source of all that we need. Describe how you depend on God daily to make provision for you.

2. "We make a good living by doing what we do," and "Our prosperous livelihood is being threatened."⁹ These statements show that Demetrius's identity was found in his occupation, success, and wealth. When we can boldly identify with who we are in Christ and not with our occupation, we no longer have to be concerned about how the message of Jesus might adversely affect our work. Describe how the message of the gospel can have a positive impact in your place of business.

Father, I thank You that my identity is in Christ alone. Holy Spirit, remind me daily of who I am in Jesus and that it is His resurrection power that lives in me. I thank You for being my source and for supplying all of my needs according to Your riches in glory. Holy Spirit, help me to work wholeheartedly unto the Lord and be unashamed of the gospel. In Jesus's name, amen.

Day 20

Acts 20

My life is worth nothing to me unless I use it for
finishing the work assigned me by the Lord Jesus.

—Acts 20:24 (NLT)

True Life

*T*hough it may seem self-deprecating for Paul to regard his life as being worthless or of little value, in truth his statement is revelatory of the degree to which he lived in surrender to the work of the Lord Jesus. His gaze vehemently fixed on the grand scheme of eternity, Paul embraced the "imprisonment and suffering that await[ed] [him]" in the very near future.[1] When our senses are flooded with the reality of suffering's looming presence, looking beyond the present moment and staring into eternity redirects our focus from this visible realm to an invisible one, a realm in which there exists a God intrinsically involved in the orchestration of our lives—taking what was meant for harm and turning it for good.[2]

Paul's faith and trust in the Lord, developed and refined "in every season by serving [Him],"[3] provided restful assurance that the ministry commissioned him by the Lord Jesus would produce fruit that would endure even unto death and beyond.[4] This sort of surrender was strongly implored by Jesus in Matthew 10:39: "…But those who let go of their lives for My sake and surrender it all to Me will discover true life." Tangible evidence of trying to live (and operate) apart from Jesus—and not in *complete* and *true* surrender to His Lordship—manifests in the form of fear, anxiety, depression, suicidal thoughts and tendencies, and other mental health disorders. Intense and stress-inducing situations will tempt you to reclaim control of your life from the Sovereign Lord. In such moments, cease all attempts at trying to preserve your life (your reputation, business, ministry, outcomes, etc.) in the traditional sense, and cast all your cares upon the One who cares for you (1 Peter 5:7).[5]

In the same manner of trusting and believing as did the apostle Paul, true reliance upon and surrender to the Lord must at some point extend beyond what we profess with our mouths and become the place of power from which we live (1 Corinthians 4:20).[6] This can only be achieved through receiving "God's [precious and undeserved] grace" by the power of His Holy Spirit which sets us free from striving and grants us life.[7] Determine in your heart today to lead a sacrificial existence in submission to the Lord Jesus, for it is only when you are willing to lay down your life in surrender to Him that you will discover true life.

Reflection Questions

1. As believers we are not to focus on our troubles. Our present troubles are small and won't last very long. For the things we see now will soon be gone, but the things we cannot see will last forever.[8] How is your faith strengthened as you redirect your focus on God's promise to cause everything to work together for your good?

2. True fulfillment in life comes only when we surrender our service to the Lord, because without Jesus we can do nothing.[9] He causes us to prosper and excel in every season of our lives because what we do for the Lord is never useless or wasted.[10] What fruits have been produced in your life as a result of your full surrender to the Lord?

Father, I thank you that my light afflictions, which are only for a moment, are working in me a far greater and eternal weight of glory. All things are working together for my good because I love you and have been called according to Your purpose. I thank You that Your word says if I let go of my life and surrender it all to You I will discover true life. There is nothing I can do for you that will ever be useless or wasted. Thank you for producing spiritual fruit in my life that is evident in my joy, peace, love and soundness of mind. In Jesus's name, amen.

Day 21

Acts 21

May the will of the Lord be done.

—Acts 21:14 (TPT)

A Spoken Word

$\mathcal{A}$ principal aim of the Holy Spirit is to communicate the Father's will to creation through what is often referred to as a prophetic word. Jesus taught in John 16:13 that the Holy Spirit would tell of "what is yet to come." This is exemplified through the life of Paul upon receiving revelation concerning the Father's will for him in the city of Jerusalem. Not knowing what would happen to him there, only that hardships and imprisonment were awaiting his arrival, Paul was compelled by the Holy Spirit to go anyway.[1] This was later confirmed by the Holy Spirit through a man named Agabus.[2] Concerned for his well-being, "the local believers all begged Paul not to go on to Jerusalem."[3]

Though oftentimes well-meaning, the relationships you have with others can greatly impact their ability to speak into your life objectively. Their fears or genuine concerns for your well-being can become intermingled in their witness. Exercising discernment and learning to distinguish the voice of the Lord from the voice of those around you is critical when discovering God's will for your life. Failure to do so may result in discouragement from pursuing the perfect plan He has for you. Acquiring wisdom is achieved in "listening to advice and accepting instruction," and while it is important to seek wise counsel, remember that it is "the purpose of the Lord that will stand."[4]

As people, we are flawed and hold great potential for error. The word of God reminds us that "there is nothing perfect in this imperfect world except [His] words."[5] Often what God reveals in part will not make sense in our natural minds and will require faith to believe for what is not yet seen. When we come into agreement with God's word,

NORKA JENKINS & TAYLER JENKINS

our faith will pull His promises into being. Maybe you are uncertain if you have indeed heard from the Lord. The wisdom of God commands that we "test the spirits to see whether they are from God."[6] This can be achieved practically in asking the Lord to confirm what He has spoken through His written word (the Bible), a scripturally supported word of advice from a trusted spiritual advisor, or by simply granting you His peace that surpasses understanding.

As difficult as it may at times be to believe, hold on for dear life to the word He has spoken to you in the presence of doubt and unbelief. The Lord longs to tell you "remarkable secrets you do not know about things to come."[7] Position yourself and your heart to hear what He is speaking to you today.

Reflection Questions

1. The Holy Spirit, the Spirit of Truth, speaks to us only what He hears from the Father and reveals prophetically what is to come.[8] Paul was warned by the Holy Spirit that chains and afflictions were prepared for him in Jerusalem.[9] The word he received was also confirmed through a prophet. What are some ways God gives you confirmation of what He has spoken to you?

2. When we receive a spoken word from God, it may not always resonate with the people in our lives. Although the believers prophesied what the Holy Spirit had already spoken to Paul in the previous chapter, they then begged him not to go to Jerusalem. How has the opinions of others discouraged you from listening to God's voice?

Father, thank You for Your Holy Spirit that guides me into all truth and tells me about the future. Help me to discern your voice clearly. I thank You that You will always give me confirmation of what You have spoken to me. Regardless of what others may say, I am committed to following Your will for my life. I have made up my mind to listen to Your voice. Thank You for always encouraging me and giving me the grace to stay on path. Not my will but Your will be done. In Jesus's name, amen.

Day 22

Acts 22

So now what are you waiting for? Get up, be baptized,
and wash away your sins as you call upon His name.

—Acts 22:16 (TPT)

The Power of Receiving Forgiveness

*T*he life of the apostle Paul reflects the power of genuine and sincere repentance born of prayerful sorrow and receiving forgiveness in Christ. Put simply, to repent is to turn away from sin and to live a life transformed into the image of Christ by the power and grace of the Holy Spirit. A true encounter with the glory and splendor of Jesus has the power to transform a murderous zealot and impassioned enforcer of the law into a fearless apostle, teacher, and preacher of the gospel of grace. Paul always had an ardent desire to please God, even before coming to know Christ.[1] Aware of this, Jesus revealed Himself to Paul and offered him salvation in His name.

Imagine if salvation had been the end-all and be-all for Paul. What if he had been satisfied in his salvation alone? Perhaps he never would have been driven to change his pattern of behavior and would have continued in his sin (persecuting Christians). It would not make much sense, would it? What would have been the purpose of his salvation? He would have still been living a life blind to the newfound grace and freedom from sin now being offered him through a relationship with Jesus. We sometimes may choose to remain in bondage to sin as a result of guilt and shame, although Christ has offered us the opportunity to live a life of freedom in Him. God's purpose in saving us does not extend only to an invitation into Heaven, rather His ultimate desire for us is to be conformed to the image and likeness of His Son, Jesus.[2]

God saved you for the glory and purposes of His kingdom. Your mistakes have not disqualified you from this heavenly call. Before the initial beating of your heart, God created you in your innermost being[3] and set you apart for His plans and purposes.[4] Fully aware of every mistake you would ever make—past, present, and future—He saw fit to choose you anyway. God loves and accepts you just as you are, and as an extension of that love He desires to see you blossom into all He has created for you to be. The loving forgiveness of the Lord found Saul and transformed him into the apostle Paul, whose ministry was instrumental in the Gentiles receiving the message of salvation in Christ. Allow the transforming power of the Holy Spirit to have His perfect work in you. No one is beyond the Lord's reach. Romans 5:8 reminds us that "while we were still sinners, Christ died for us." We cannot escape this inexplicable depth of love and forgiveness that has been offered to us.

Paul so fully received the Lord's forgiveness of his past that he was able to stand before a crowd of witnesses and share the testimony of his life in honor of God's transformative glory. Not gripped by shame or regret, he understood the significance of his salvation in the grand scheme of the Lord's glorious plan to reach the Gentiles. In the same way, your testimony holds the potential to draw an entirely new generation of believers unto Christ. Do not wallow in the shame of your past; surrender all that you are to the Lord and receive His forgiveness for your every mistake. Allow the gospel of grace to produce hope, redemption, and transformation in you and in the body of Christ for generations to come.

Reflection Questions

1. We were designed by God to feel remorse over our sin. Our remorse produces repentance and provokes an eagerness to do what is right.[5] The Holy Spirit gives us the desire and the power to do what pleases God.[6] How has your remorse over sin transformed you?

2. By the power of the Holy Spirit, we receive forgiveness and are released from the guilt of our sin.[7] We no longer live with shame and regret, because there is no condemnation for those who are in Christ Jesus who walk according to the Spirit.[8] How has this truth of freedom changed your life?

Father, You have designed me to feel remorse over my sin in order to produce repentance that leads to victory in my life, and I am eager to do what is right by You. By the power of Your Holy Spirit, I receive Your forgiveness. Because I walk according to the Spirit and not according to my flesh, I am no longer condemned. I thank You that I am the righteousness of God in Christ Jesus and I have been set free of guilt and shame. In Jesus's name, amen.

Day 23

Acts 23

For you sit there judging me according to the law, yet you
broke the law when you ordered me to be struck.

—Acts 23:3 (TPT)

Is There Something in Your Eye?

*M*any people have heard the words, "Do not judge, or you too will be judged," uttered at one point or another.[1] Though widely known and generally accepted as a universal truth, the arbitrary and common usage of this verse can drown out its true power and meaning. There are eternal consequences to the hypocrisy that accompanies judgmental thoughts and attitudes. Paul, confronting the high priest, warned that God would strike him on account of his judgment and hypocrisy.[2] Comparably, if we judge others "unfairly with an attitude of self-righteous superiority," we too will be judged according to the same measure by The Ultimate Judiciary.[3] We must continually lay our hearts bare before the Father and rely on the power of His Holy Spirit to convict us of "sinful[ly] unrepentant" judgmental thoughts and attitudes.[4] A heart postured in humility is the only suitable dwelling place for the Spirit of God.[5]

There is a delicate, equilibrium balance that we must learn to maintain in order to preserve the integrity of God's truth without passing judgment on others. Do not allow the fear of being labelled judgmental cause you to shy away from speaking the truth concerning the word of God in love. We have been "solemnly charged in the presence of God and of Christ Jesus, who is to judge the living and the dead …, [to] preach the word as an official messenger."[6] Employ discernment as you are led by the Holy Spirit in choosing the right time to correct "those who err in doctrine or behavior, warn [those who sin], [and] exhort and encourage [those who are growing toward spiritual maturity]."[7]

If you express genuine and heartfelt concern for another believer, prayerfully consult the Holy Spirit concerning what you should do. Secondly, if no relationship exists between you and the individual for whom you are concerned, seek to establish one. Take the time to get to know people as they are before trying to change them. If prompted by the Holy Spirit, be a vessel through which God can speak His truth into their situation. Pray with such an individual and ask the Holy Spirit to usher in guidance with wisdom from above. *True* wisdom from above is "unwavering without [self-righteous] hypocrisy [and self-serving guile]."[8] Do not intermingle your opinion with the word of God; for such is the difference between truth and error, good advice and godly counsel, true love and hateful judgment. Lastly, ask the Holy Spirit to conduct a thorough heart search, making you aware of any judgment that may be hidden deep within your heart. In doing so, we position ourselves to first remove the log from our own eye so we can see clearly enough to remove the speck from our brother's eye.[9]

Following the model set by our Lord and Savior Jesus Christ, intercede for the redemption of lost souls to be reconciled to a loving relationship with God the Father. Be a bridge builder, not a stumbling block, as you encourage other believers on the path toward righteousness. God sent forth His truth into the world endowed with all the power, love, mercy, and grace of heaven in hopes of redeeming the lost. Let us stand for His mission and become wholehearted ministers of His truth and of His grace.

Reflection Questions

1. "We will be treated as we treat others. The standard we use in judging is the standard by which we will be judged."[10] Judging others leads us into hypocrisy. When have you criticized someone for their actions, only to find in your conduct the same attitude or behavior that you judged?

2. We cannot be effective in our ministry to others if we have not yet addressed our hypocrisies. Jesus tells us to first acknowledge our own blind spots and deal with them before we are to deal with those of our friends.[11] What are the blind spots in your life that need to be dealt with?

Father, I thank You for sending Your Son, Jesus into the world not to judge the world, but to save the world. I ask for forgiveness of any judgments and criticisms that may be in my heart. I will not judge others and become a stumbling block that causes them to fall. I thank You that Your wisdom is always pure, filled with peace, considerate, and teachable. It is also filled with love and never displays prejudice or hypocrisy in any form. Holy Spirit, give me the wisdom to know when an opportunity is favorable to correct, warn, or encourage those growing toward spiritual maturity and discernment to know the difference. In Jesus's name, amen.

Day 24

Acts 24

Felix became terrified and said, "Leave me for now. I'll send for you later when it's more convenient."

—Acts 24:25 (TPT)

Finding the Time

*I*t can be easy to disregard the intangible promises of God as pipe dreams that we hope to maybe someday see fulfilled at a more convenient hour. This was the case of Governor Felix during the period of the apostle Paul's trial versus the Jewish elders. Felix desired to understand more pertaining to the knowledge of Christ and the Kingdom of God. However, when came the opportunity for repentance and salvation, the governor shrunk back in fear waiting for a more opportune time. Despite two years of accumulating much knowledge concerning "the Way" through Paul's witness, Felix ultimately failed to place the full weight of his trust in Christ.

Hebrews 3:12 in the Amplified Bible defines an unbelieving heart as one "which refuses to trust and rely on the Lord" and can actually result in "turning away from the Living God." Felix's unbelieving heart delayed the promise of salvation from being fully realized in his life. Our inability to trust in the Lord and His word is one reason we may experience delay in seeing His promises fulfilled in our lives. Fear and unbelief are strategies the enemy employs to rob you of your destiny. Consider the desires of your heart, placed there by God, and whether or not you have lost hope for the coming of those dreams. Hope deferred makes the heart sick[1], but the hope we place into the hands of Jesus will not by any means lead to disappointment.[2]

The Holy Spirit placed before Felix repeated opportunities for him to surrender to the promise of salvation. A hardened heart consumed with greed and the cares of this world choked out the seeds of promise and hope, never to take root in his heart. As a result, a more "convenient time" never came.[3] "Today [while there is still opportunity], if you hear His voice, do not harden your heart."[4] There is no better time to accomplish your dreams than right now. Jesus has promised you life in abundance, and that life begins today.[5] Confidently trust in and rely on God to bring to pass those promises He has placed in you—both in His time and in His way. Consult the Holy Spirit for wisdom and strategy concerning the practical steps you can take on your way to destiny. What are you waiting for? There's never been a better time than now.

Reflection Questions

1. Felix had an accurate *understanding* about the Way of Jesus, but he did not have *faith* in Christ. Upon hearing about righteousness and the coming day of judgment, Felix became frightened. Fear keeps us bound by unbelief. How has fear and unbelief kept you from placing your full faith in God?

2. When will you find the time? Over a period of two years, Felix often sent for Paul and spoke with him, but his concerns for other things (money, pleasing the Jewish people, etc.) crowded out the message of Jesus. Explain how the cares of this world can prevent the word of God from taking root in your heart.

Father, I ask that Your Holy Spirit keep my heart from fear, unbelief, and turning away from You. When I hear Your voice, I pray that the worries of this world, the deceitfulness of wealth, and the desires for all other things don't settle in to choke out Your word, causing it to be unfruitful in my life. Thank You for keeping Your promises and being patient with me because You desire for me to turn away from my sin. In Jesus's name, amen.

Acts 25

Paul said by the Holy Spirit, "I have done nothing wrong."

—Acts 25:8 (TPT)

Not Guilty

here is an accuser who stands in the courtroom of heaven day in and out, making vicious accusations against us before God the Father.[1] A striking portrayal of this reality was once illustrated when "religious authorities and prominent leaders among the Jews brought formal charges against Paul before Festus."[2] Though they "encircled him and leveled against him many serious charges …they were unable to substantiate."[3] Empowered by the Holy Spirit with remarkable revelation concerning Christ's sacrifice, Paul was able to boldly profess his innocence in the face of his accusers, his defense rooted in this timeless truth: "Therefore there is now no condemnation [no guilty verdict, no punishment] for those who are in Christ Jesus."[4]

The enemy is in relentless pursuit against the joy of your salvation and, ultimately, your life. Likewise, you too must be relentless— empowered by the Holy Spirit—to stand strong, persevere, and press into the Lord's presence through prayer. Plain, stale, old religion does not stand a chance against the spiritual war that rages on in the unseen realm. The reality of Christ Jesus's resurrection must be manifested in your innermost being in order to secure victory over the enemy. When Jesus suffered a sinner's death on the cross at Calvary, He fulfilled all requirements of the law of sin and death, and being raised to life again, Jesus granted us new life under the law of the Spirit in Him.[5]

When your accusers attempt to hold you captive to the law of sin as a result of your past mistakes, humbly proclaim with wholehearted conviction that you are innocent of all charges. By the blood of Jesus, all of sin's debts have been paid. God the Father is the ultimate judge, and Jesus is your perfect defender. He rushes to your defense before

Norka Jenkins & Tayler Jenkins

the enemy's tireless accusations. As in the case of Paul, allow the Holy Spirit to call to your remembrance the truth concerning your salvation in Christ Jesus. Jesus rendered Himself an offering for the transgressions of the world eternally. In turn, His hope for us is that we would choose to live according to the power of His Holy Spirit and not according to the flesh.[6] Allow the spiritual significance of Christ's life, death, and resurrection to come alive in you. We overcome the accuser by the blood of the Lamb and the word of our testimony.[7]

Reflection Questions

1. Paul said by the Holy Spirit and in the face of his accusers, "I've done nothing wrong." There is an adversary that is persistent in bringing accusations of sinful behavior against us—but Jesus died on the cross, paid the penalty for sin, and therefore we are no longer guilty. The guilt and power of sin has been condemned! How has this revelation of truth transformed your life?

2. Jesus has liberated us from the law of sin and death, and we are free to live by the power of the Holy Spirit. The mindset controlled by the Spirit finds peace and life and empowers us. We no longer live under the impulses of our human nature; we are habitually putting to death the sinful deeds of the body. What are you habitually putting into practice today in order to produce righteous living in the Spirit?

Father, thank You that there is no condemnation for those who are in Christ Jesus. My old nature has passed away, and I am a new creation. I have put off my old sinful nature and my former way of life, and I am being renewed in the spirit of my mind. I thank You for sending Your son, Jesus to pay the penalty of death for me so that I may live. Holy Spirit, empower me daily to walk in righteousness and to exemplify a life that brings glory to the Father. In Jesus's name, amen.

Day 26

Acts 26

But God has protected me right up to this present time so
I can testify to everyone, from the least to greatest.

—Acts 26:22 (TPT)

Your Testimony

In the previous chapter, we uncovered the way to overcome the accuser of the brethren: by the blood of the Lamb and the word of our testimony.[1] While the enemy seeks to hold us hostage to the past, the Lord not only desires to set us free, but also to strengthen and empower us through His grace to share our story as a testament to His goodness and redemptive power. Before King Agrippa and a crowd of witnesses, the apostle Paul testified to the way the Lord transformed his life in order to reveal "[his] destiny and to commission [him] as [His] assistant."[2] With "confidence and boldness," Paul spoke of what the Lord had accomplished through his life and ministry.[3] In simply sharing what God had done, Paul nearly persuaded King Agrippa to become a Christian.[4]

Most basically, your testimony is the story of how you came to accept Christ as your personal Lord and Savior. Your willingness to share your testimony is critical for the continued growth and expansion of the kingdom of God on earth and for pointing lost souls to the hope of salvation in Christ. The prospect of evangelizing the gospel of Jesus Christ in this way is intimidating to some for a plethora of reasons. Regardless of any potential hesitation, we have been charged to revere Christ as Lord in our hearts.[5] As such, we must always be prepared to give an answer, with gentleness and respect, to everyone who asks the reason for the hope that we have.[6] Prepare to be questioned in regard to your salvation, as you reflect on the events leading up to your decision to believe in Jesus Christ as Lord.

Romans 10:14-17 challenges our regard for the hope of salvation for the lost: "How, then, can they call on the one they have not believed in? And how can they believe in the one they have not heard? And how can they hear without someone preaching to them? And how can anyone preach unless they are sent?" We have been sent by Jesus to "go and make disciples of many nations."[7] The decision to follow the internal promptings of the Holy Spirit and tell your story might be the only opportunity some people will ever have to hear the message of the gospel. Sharing your testimony is one of the most practical ways to connect with people on a personal level and introduce them to the hope of a life devoted to Christ. The events of your life have been unfolding to produce in you a unique anointing that is purposed to draw a dark world to the light of salvation found only in Christ. With all boldness and authority in Jesus, the apostle Paul did not love his life so much as to renounce his faith, despite the great potential for loss it held for him.[8] In the same way, testify shamelessly before mankind of the wonderful things God has done for you.

Reflection Questions

1. "Everyone who acknowledges me publicly here on earth. I will also acknowledge before my Father in heaven. But everyone who denies me here on earth, I will also deny before my Father in heaven."[9] What has prevented you from sharing the message of the gospel?

2. We should always be ready to explain our faith when anyone asks about the hope living within us. Paul presented evidence to the court as to how his encounter with Jesus transformed his life. However, as believers, some of us have not yet shared our faith in Christ. How can you be more intentional about sharing your testimony?

Father, I thank You for my faith in Jesus. Reveal to me if I have any resistance in my heart to share how You have changed my life. Holy Spirit, I ask You to help me to walk in boldness and in Your wisdom as I live before unbelievers. I will make it my duty to make Jesus known. How can He be made known if I do not share? I've been commanded to go and make disciples of all nations, so I pray that every word I speak be drenched with grace and tempered with truth and clarity. Then I will be ready to give a respectful answer to anyone that asks about my faith. In Jesus's name, amen.

Day 27

Acts 27

After many days of seeing neither the sun nor the stars, and
with the violent storm continuing to rage against us, all
hope of ever getting through it alive was abandoned.

—Acts 27:20 (TPT)

Dry Ground

Cast into the open sea amid gale force winds, the apostle Paul was faced with mounting opposition on his way to Rome, where he was destined to stand trial before Caesar. In the middle of the storm, Paul maintained supernatural peace and exhibited unwavering trust in the Lord his God. What is your response when the storms of life come? In avoiding the potential for calamity, do you attempt to set course for a more desirable position or do you, against all odds of survival, choose to remain still in faith?[1] In our natural minds, the decision to "remain" does not make much sense. However, through our eyes of faith, we know and have experienced firsthand that they who "wait on the Lord" and renew their strength are those who have mastered the art of waiting.[2] Even in the face of mounting opposition, the word of the Lord remains true. After "all hope of ever getting through [the storm] alive was abandoned," the angel of the Lord appeared before Paul and commanded him not to be afraid.[3] He assured Paul he would live to stand trial before Caesar and that, because of the favor of God on his life, all the lives of those sailing with him would be preserved.[4]

A large part of spiritual discernment is the ability to recognize the Lord's hand of favor upon you even in the midst of less than desirable circumstances. Your commitment to the Lord in every season has awarded you His favor that extends to those around you. When you have surrendered to the Lord's sovereignty, what was meant by the enemy to breed harm and destruction God will use to usher you into a new place of destiny. "As fire tests gold and purifies it," so do trials test our faith for the ultimate purpose of bringing praise, honor, and glory to the Lord Jesus.[5] Resting in the Lord's promise of their survival, Paul was able to encourage the sailors who were in constant suspense and had gone nearly fourteen days without food. Beware the crippling effects of fear, distracting you from the need to care for yourself and your basic responsibilities.[6] When all seems despairing, a lack of nourishment or regard for self-care can be detrimental. Rely on the Lord's grace to care for your physical and spiritual needs in the middle of the storm, and encourage others to do the same.

Hope in the Lord when all seems hopeless. Just as the sailors cut away their anchors heading towards the shore, so too must we cut away anchors to anything apart from our hope in the Lord. No matter what you are facing today or what awaits you tomorrow, it is not over until God says so. God has not brought you this far to leave you. You *will* survive the storm. Stay the course, and continue to trust God to deliver you once again to dry ground.

Reflection Questions

1. The intensity of our storms can make it difficult to stay on the course where God is taking us. When we have no control and all hope is gone, the Holy Spirit protects us and tells us not to be afraid. Paul believed God's promise of protection and was empowered to encourage those traveling with him. How do you anchor to hope in Jesus when you go through difficult seasons, and does it flow to those walking with you?

2. Those traveling with Paul were so worried that they had not eaten for two weeks. The anxiety caused by our circumstances can sometimes cause us to neglect basic responsibilities, but God grants us His grace and promises to give us peace. As you stand still and wait on God's perfect timing to deliver you from the storm onto dry ground, what are some practical ways you can sustain your peace and not be paralyzed by the storm?

Father, Jesus said that here on earth I would have trials but to take heart because He has overcome the world. Holy Spirit, endow me with wisdom and strategy as I navigate through the difficult seasons in my life. I thank You for supernatural peace, joy, and perseverance, and for using this to strengthen my faith. Help me to remember to also speak encouragement and hope to those around me in the midst of my storm. In Jesus's name, amen.

Day 28

Acts 28

For your hearts are hard and insensitive to me—you must be hard of hearing! For you've closed your eyes so that you won't be troubled by the truth, and you've covered your ears so you won't have to listen and be pierced by what I say. For then you would have to respond and repent, so that I could heal your hearts.

—Acts 28:27 (TPT)

A New Heart

*I*t can be overwhelming to consider the troubling condition of our world today. Learning of wars, famine, pandemics, religious persecution, every form of injustice, and moral declination, we can slowly begin to adopt a cold and callous perspective on life. In Matthew 24:10, Jesus prophesied that, as a result of the "increase of sin and lawlessness[,] hearts that once burned with passion for God and others will grow cold." In light of this prophetic revelation, the Lord desires to heal the hearts of His people.

In order to be an effective ambassador for Christ during perilous times, we need the unveiled truth of God to produce a change in us to be imparted to the rest of the world. A stone-cold heart inhibits the light of revelation and truth from piercing our innermost being. The Lord desires a most holy exchange: our heart of stone for a new heart of flesh.[1] An outpouring of the Lord's Spirit guides us along paths of righteousness. We then become conduits of His love and creative power to produce the heavenly change in the world that we long to see.

Being conformed to the image of Christ and transformed by the renewing of our minds is the only way to remain steadfast in our convictions as we seek to draw those who are lost and hurting.[2] We must abide in the presence of the Lord and continually examine our hearts for traces of indifference or callousness pertaining to the perishing state of our world. The redemptive love of Christ desires that no man should perish, and it is the driving force in presenting "the truth to everyone in the sight and presence of God."[3] While we can sow seeds of truth, it is only the power of the Holy Spirit that can guide mankind into all truth.[4] Our world is in dire need of a spiritual awakening that comes on the coattails of new revelation.

Do not be satisfied with a form of godliness, but hunger and thirst after the transformational power of God's kingdom. Do not shy away from the Lord's truth, for it is the revelation of God's truth that keeps us from becoming like the unbeliever who is blind to the image of Christ.[5] Revelation truth cannot penetrate a cold heart. Allow God to heal your heart so that you may see and perceive revelation of His truth for His kingdom's glory.

Reflection Questions

1. Jesus commands, "Love each other just as much as I have loved you." He also warns us that because of the increase in sin and lawlessness, the love of most people will grow cold. Feelings of indifference toward a hurting and broken world is a sign that our capacity to love as God does is diminishing. How has the current condition of the world negatively impacted your ability to love others?

2. A hardened heart is non-responsive and perishing, and it prevents the full truth of the gospel from being revealed to us. It is a heart that cannot understand. The Holy Spirit, the Spirit of Truth, comes to unveil the reality of every truth within us. Explain how a cold and hardened heart can distort your ability to fully comprehend what is true.

Father, I thank You for the truth and revelation of Your word. I ask that You create in me a clean heart and renew a right spirit within me. You have commanded me to love others just as You have loved me. I thank You for taking my stubborn heart and giving me a heart that is tender, responsive, and filled with Your Spirit. I thank You that I am not blinded by the god of this age, but when I hear You speak I understand, and when I see You move I comprehend. Father, I will turn my heart to You so that my heart can be healed. In Jesus's name, amen.

References

Chapter 1:

The Wait

1   Acts 1:3

2   Acts 1:2, 4

3   Acts 1:14

4   Hebrews 10:25

5   1 Thessalonians 5:17

Chapter 2:

The Promise of the Holy Spirit

1   Acts 2:4

2   Acts 1:4

3   1 Corinthians 12:11

Chapter 3:

I'll Give You What I Have

1   Acts 3:16

2   1 Corinthians 12:4

3   2 Corinthians 9:11

4   Mark 5:34

5   Proverbs 11:25

6   Ephesians 3:20

7   1 Corinthians 12:7

8   Acts 3:9–10

9   2 Corinthians 9:12

Chapter 4:

Extraordinary Boldness

1   Acts 4:13

2   1 Timothy 4:12

3   1 Corinthians 1:27

4   2 Corinthians 3:5

5   2 Timothy 1:7

6   Acts 4:29–30

7   Acts 4:13

8   2 Corinthians 3:5

9   Matthew 18:19

10   Acts 4:29, 31

Chapter 5:

Nothing Can Stop You

1   Acts 5:29

2   Acts 5:41

3   Joshua 1:9

4   1 Corinthians 10:13

5   Isaiah 59:19

6   2 Corinthians 4:17

7   Proverbs 3:6

8   Philippians 1:6

9   Matthew 28:19–20

10   Acts 5:40–41

11   Acts 5:38–39

12   Acts 5:29

5   1 Peter 3:15

6   1 Peter 3:15

7   Matthew 28:18–19

8   Revelation 12:11 (AMP)

9   Matthew 10:32–33

Chapter 27:

Dry Ground

1   Acts 27:10

2   Isaiah 40:31

3   Acts 27:24

4   Acts 27:24–25

5   1 Peter 1:7–9

6   Acts 27:33–34

Chapter 28:

A New Heart

1   Ezekiel 36:26

2   Romans 12:2

3   2 Corinthians 4:2

4   John 16:13

5   2 Corinthians 4:4

About the Author

Norka Jenkins is a wife, mother of three, and career professional in the Greater Houston area. She gave her life to Christ as a young adult in 1992 and has served in ministry in various capacities over the past 28 years. In 2004, Norka and her husband Ty relocated from California to Houston shortly after receiving a word from God to sell their home and move to Texas. Her life has since been devoted to growing in her service to the Lord, her family and her ministry in the marketplace. Norka's desire is to help young believers grow deeper in their knowledge of Jesus, know their identity in Christ, discern truth, and walk in their unique purpose with boldness and authority empowered by the Holy Spirit. Norka hopes to establish a legacy of faith that contributes to the growth and edification of the body of Christ for generations to come.

Tayler Jenkins is a gifted writer, performer and choreographer whose creative works emphasize her love and passion for fusing faith with artistry as a means of inspiring confidence and establishing a sense of purpose in the lives of those she touches. After graduating from Texas State University with a degree in dance performance and choreography, she founded Anthem Performing Arts Studios, a non-profit organization devoted to equipping and empowering the rising generation of performing artists with foundational tools and principles needed to forge long-term success both in their artform and in their faith. For more information, visit anthemstudios.org. Currently, Tayler is on staff part-time at her local church where she faithfully serves congregants as they aspire to go deeper in their knowledge and relationship with the Lord.

Printed in the United States
by Baker & Taylor Publisher Services